SPEAKING EFFECTIVELY
A GUIDE FOR AIR FORCE SPEAKERS

by

JOHN A. KLINE

Air University Press
Maxwell Air Force Base, Alabama

December 1989

Library of Congress Cataloging-in-Publication Data

Kline, John A.
    Speaking Effectively: A Guide for Air Force Speakers/by John A. Kline.
            p. cm.
    "December 1989."
    1. Public speaking.   I. Title.
    PN4121.K67   1989
    808.5'1 — dc20   89-78063
                                          CIP
    ISBN 978-1-58566-031-5

                    First Printing January 1990
                    Second Printing September 1990
                    Third Printing June 1994
                    Fourth Printing June 1995
                    Fifth Printing June 1996
                    Sixth Printing August 2001
                    Seventh Printing April 2003
                    Eighth Printing September 2004
                    Ninth Printing August 2005
                    Tenth Printing November 2005
                    Eleventh Printing March 2007
                    Twelfth Printing August 2007
                    Thirteenth Printing April 2008
                    Fourteenth Printing August 2008
                    Fifteenth Printing June 2010

Disclaimer

Air University Press
Air Force Research Institute
155 N. Twining Street
Maxwell AFB AL 36112-6026
http://aupress.au.af.mil

CONTENTS

Chapter		Page
	DISCLAIMER	ii
	FOREWORD	vii
	ABOUT THE AUTHOR	ix
	PREFACE	xi
1	PREPARING TO TALK	1
	Types of Speaking	2
	Briefing	2
	Teaching Lecture	2
	Speech	3
	Audience	3
	Audience Analysis	4
	Audience Attitude	5
	Subject	6
	Selecting the Subject	6
	Narrowing the Subject	8
	Choosing a Title	8
	Objectives	9
	General Responses	9
	Specific Responses	9
	Gathering Material	10
	Self	10
	Others	11
	Library	12
	Evaluating Material	12
2	ORGANIZING THE TALK	13
	Time	14
	Space	15
	Cause/Effect	16
	Problem/Solution	17
	Pro/Con	18
	Topical	19
	Combining Patterns	20
	Now that You Have Organized	22

Chapter		*Page*

3 SUPPORTING THE TALK 23
   Factors to Consider 24
      Briefing 24
      Teaching Lecture 24
      Speech 24
   Logical Thinking 25
      Slanted Reasoning 25
      Irrational Appeals 26
   Verbal Support 27
      Definitions 27
      Examples 28
      Comparisons 30
      Testimony 31
      Statistics 31
      Humor 34
   Visual Support 36
      Suggestions 36
      Using a Chalkboard 38
   After You Have Your Support 38

4 BEGINNING AND ENDING THE TALK 41
   Briefing 41
      Introduction 42
      Conclusion 42
   Teaching Lecture 42
      Introduction 43
      Conclusion 44
   Speech 45
      Introduction 45
      Conclusion 47
   Suggestions for Gaining Attention 48
      Question 48
      Quotation 49
      Joke 50
      Startling Statement 50
      Gimmick 50
      Common Ground 51
      Reference 51
   Transitions and Interim Summaries 53
      Transitions 53
      Interim Summaries 54
   After Preparation, Then What? 54

Chapter		Page
5	PRESENTING A TALK	55
	Methods of Presentation	55
	Memorizing	56
	Manuscript Reading	56
	Impromptu	59
	Extemporaneous	59
	Keyword Outline	60
	Nervousness	63
	Suggestions for Nervous Speakers	64
	Physical Behavior	65
	Eye Contact	65
	Body Movement	66
	Gestures	67
	Use of Voice	68
	Quality	69
	Intelligibility	69
	Variety	70
	Sincerity	71

FOREWORD

Dr Kline's book, *Speaking Effectively*, is an essential resource for anyone faced with any kind of speaking situation. It contains hints, anecdotal examples, and the accumulated wisdom of decades of speaking experience. John is highly regarded in government, religious, and corporate circles and widely in demand because he is a great speaker and because he can help anyone communicate more effectively. He brings that expertise forward in a way that both teaches and entertains.

First published in 1989 and currently in its fourth printing, *Speaking Effectively* teaches speakers throughout the Air Force and in other federal agencies the art of captivating an audience. From preparation of your talk through delivery, this straightforward book takes you step-by-step through the stages of effectively developing and presenting briefings, lectures, and speeches.

This book includes such essential principles of effective delivery as speaking clearly, at the right pace for your audience and subject, and loud enough for all to hear, but not too loud. Yet it also covers less obvious, but equally essential, principles such as a speaker's nonverbal signals, which can make or break a presentation.

I strongly recommend Dr Kline's book whether you are a novice or an experienced speaker. It will help the novice begin developing time-proven speaking techniques, and it will help more experienced speakers continue perfecting the skills needed to grab and hold an audience.

JAY W. KELLEY
Lieutenant General, USAF
Commander, Air University

ABOUT THE AUTHOR

Dr. John A. Kline

Dr John A. Kline is a senior executive (SES) and Academic Provost for Air University. He received his BS from Iowa State University. He held an NDEA Fellowship while earning MS and PhD degrees at the University of Iowa.

Dr Kline was professor of communication at the universities of New Mexico and Missouri–Columbia. He has been at Air University since 1975 as professor, dean, educational advisor, and finally as provost.

Dr Kline has written books, presented many papers, and published widely in leading professional journals. He is an accomplished speaker, he has lectured extensively throughout the Air Force and he has presented many speeches to a variety of military, professional, religious, and corporate organizations worldwide.

PREFACE

Speaking Effectively presents techniques on how to speak successfully. It takes a "how-to" approach to effective speaking in the Air Force and presents proven techniques as concisely and completely as possible. Experienced speakers will find little here that is new. Yet each speaker, no matter how skilled, needs to keep these basic techniques in mind.

The content is organized chronologically according to the steps a speaker would normally follow: preparing, organizing, choosing appropriate support material, deciding how to begin and end, and finally presenting the actual talk. Although these basic steps apply to any kind of speaking, some important variations exist to accommodate different types of Air Force speaking. Therefore, the book consistently makes distinctions among the three types of Air Force speaking: briefing, teaching lecture, and formal speech.

The book should not become a straightjacket to thinking. Nearly every principle, technique, and suggestion has exceptions. In fact, the only principle that never changes is that an effective speaker is always willing to adjust to the audience. For this reason, the other principles can be modified if the needs of the audience so dictate.

Speaking Effectively is written for the officers, enlisted personnel, and civilians who must speak in the course of performing their day-to-day Air Force business. However, the principles and techniques do not apply only to Air Force speaking. They work in all situations, and they are as old as those in Aristotle's *Rhetoric* or Cicero's *De Oratore*.

I am indebted to former teachers, students, and audiences for the content of this book. I apologize if I have used their ideas or those of other textbooks without acknowledging the source. Quite frankly, I have assimilated these ideas into my own thinking and practice, and no longer know where I learned them.

Finally, I say a special thanks to my wife, Ann, who endured my writing of this book. Even more, she has been very patient with a demanding traveling and speaking schedule that required not only time away but also time at home preparing speeches— time that I could have devoted to her.

John A. Kline

JOHN A. KLINE

CHAPTER 1

PREPARING TO TALK

Recent studies show that speaking in front of a group is by far the greatest fear of most people. It ranks ahead of the fear of dying, riding in an airplane, or failure in other areas of one's personal life.

Unless you are highly unusual, at some time in your life you have talked to a group of people and your knees began shaking, your voice quivered, your head ached, and the only dry place on your body was the inside of your mouth. Then the strange muscle spasms began. One eyelid began to twitch uncontrollably. Your

legs felt like soft rubber. And then it happened: Your memory, on its own and for no apparent reason, left you. At this point you promised yourself that you would never get yourself in this situation again.

Although the fear of speaking is common, studies show that one of the most admired qualities in others is their ability to speak in front of a group. Furthermore, other things being equal, the person who can communicate ideas clearly will be more successful. The remainder of this book is directed toward helping you be the kind of speaker others admire—the kind who gets the job done in every speaking situation.

Types of Speaking

There are several types of speaking common in the Air Force. Although most of the same general principles and techniques apply to all types, there are some differences.

Briefing

The best military briefings are concise and factual. Their major purpose is to inform—tell about a mission, operation, or concept. At times they also direct—enable listeners to perform a procedure or carry out instructions. At other times they advocate or persuade—support a certain solution and lead listeners to accept that solution. For example, a staff officer might want officers at a higher echelon to accept a certain solution. Every good briefing has the virtues of accuracy, brevity, and clarity. These are the ABCs of the briefing. Accuracy and clarity characterize all good speaking, but brevity distinguishes the briefing from other types of speaking. By definition, a briefing is brief, concise, and direct.

Teaching Lecture

Much speaking in the Air Force is directed toward teaching.

The lecture is the method of instruction most often used. As the name implies, the primary purpose of a teaching lecture is to teach or to inform students about a given subject. For convenience, teaching lectures can be divided into the following types: (1) formal lectures, where the communication is generally one-sided with no verbal participation by the students, and (2) informal lectures, usually presented to smaller audiences and allowing for verbal interaction between the instructor and students.

Speech

A speech generally has one of three basic purposes: to inform, to persuade, or to entertain. The *informative speech* is a narration concerning a specific topic but does not involve a sustained effort to teach. Speeches to civic clubs, orientation talks, and presentations at commanders' calls are examples of speeches to inform. The *persuasive speech* is designed to move an audience to belief or action on some topic, product, or other matter. Recruiting speeches to high school graduating classes, budget defenses, and courts-martial summations are all primarily speeches to persuade. The *entertaining speech* gives enjoyment to the audience. The speaker often relies on humor and vivid language as a primary means of entertaining the listeners. A speech at a dining-out may be a speech to entertain.

Audience

Talking to hear one's own voice may feed the ego and even cause self-persuasion, but whatever type of speaking you are doing, the goal should be to communicate with others. A basic assumption, then, is that all speaking should be audience-centered. Since speakers have a primary responsibility of adapting the message to the audiences, they need to know as much about their audiences as possible.

Audience Analysis

There are two reliable methods for gaining information about audiences. Used together they can be extremely useful. The first is to organize information you already have about the audience. Knowing such variables as age, sex, rank, and experience can help you relate to the audience. If one or more of these or similar variables separates you from the audience, you may want to give special attention to ways of emphasizing similarities and reducing differences.

The second method, when you have not talked to a particular group before, is to check with someone who has. Perhaps a

friend or colleague has already talked to the same group and can tell you what to expect. A local civic club regularly interrupts and heckles guest speakers. Imagine the chagrin of a speaker who is not familiar with this practice and takes the interruption and heckling personally. Granted, this audience behavior is a pretty extreme case and may not be the proper way for an audience to react. Still, it is better to know about such things before one speaks.

Audience Attitude

In the preceding instance, the uninformed speaker might assume wrongly that the audience was hostile. In some instances, you may have to face a hostile audience. An extreme example of a speaker facing a hostile audience is when the President must confront a group of militants on the White House lawn. In such circumstances, the emotions of the audience are so great that effective communication becomes very difficult.

Most likely you will never have to speak to an overly hostile audience, but you may have to speak to one that is mildly hostile either to you or to your ideas. What can you do? Assuming that you are determined to be heard and the audience is willing to give you a chance, hostility can often be overcome. Clearly, your first task as a speaker is to change the audience attitude—if not to friendliness, then at least to a more neutral position. Your chances for success are much greater if you somehow build rapport with your listeners. Often this can be done by using one or more of the following techniques:

1. Avoid behaving in a conceited or antagonistic manner.
2. Demonstrate a genuine concern for your listeners.
3. Exhibit friendliness and warmth toward your listeners.
4. Emphasize similarities between your listeners and you.
5. Be honest and straightforward.
6. Use humor that is in good taste, especially if it is at your own expense.

7. Indicate your association with people who are held in high esteem by the audience.

8. Do not let negative, nonverbal aspects of your behavior contradict what you are saying.

9. Demonstrate that you are an expert and have done your homework on the subject.

10. Refrain from stating the main idea or conclusion at the outset. Present your facts first that you and your listeners agree upon, and then build toward your conclusion.

Most audiences will be friendly. They consist of people who are, for the most part, favorably disposed toward you as a speaker. Most people want you to do a good job. Furthermore, they usually are not in violent disagreement with your point of view. An informative briefing to other members of your organization, a speech to a local civic club, and a teaching lecture in the classroom are examples of speaking before friendly audiences.

Subject

The problem of selecting a subject for a briefing or teaching lecture does not often arise in the ordinary course of Air Force business. You will seldom have to look around for something to talk about. The subjects are implicit in the work of the organization. A staff briefing, for example, arises from the need to communicate certain subject matter. A teaching lecture is given to satisfy a particular curriculum need. On the other hand, a formal speech to persuade, inform, or entertain may provide you with more latitude in selecting the subject.

Selecting the Subject

On some occasions, the subject of your speech will be determined—at least partly—by the group. A local civic club, for instance, may ask you to talk to them about a job, hobby, or community project you are heading up. At other times, the choice of the subject will be left entirely up to you. Almost always, however, you will be free to choose the particular aspect or area of your subject that you wish to emphasize. There are several questions you can ask yourself about the subject or aspect of the subject you choose to talk about:

1. Is this the best subject I can think of? Certainly this is a tough question. But you can answer it more wisely if you consider a number of subjects. As a rule, a carefully selected subject or aspect of the subject chosen after some thought will be a better choice than the "straw-clutching" effect that characterizes many searches for suitable subjects.

2. Is this a subject that I already know something about and can find more? If not, then perhaps you should search elsewhere. There is no substitute for complete and authoritative knowledge of the subject.

3. Am I interested in the subject? If you are not interested in what you will be talking about, you will find preparation a dull task, and you will have difficulty in capturing the interest of the audience. Talking about a community service project on which you have spent many hours or a new program that you have helped implement on the job is probably much closer to your heart than a subject that you found while searching through a list of suggested topics.

4. Is the subject suitable for my audience? Does it fit their intellectual capacity? Is it a subject that they will be interested in? A subject may be suitable or interesting to an audience if it vitally concerns their well-being, offers solutions to a problem they have, is new or timely, or if there is a conflict of opinion about it.

5. Can the subject or aspect of the subject be discussed adequately in the time I have? One of the greatest problems many speakers have is that they fail to narrow their subject. Because of this problem, they generally do one of two things: (a) they don't adequately cover the subject, or (b) they talk too long. Both results are bad.

Narrowing the Subject

Some subjects are so broad or complex that you cannot possibly do justice to them in a single speech. In ten minutes you cannot tell much about "Soviet Industry," but perhaps you can adequately cover "The Iron Industry of the Soviet Union" or "Steel Production in the Urals." Speakers often tackle subjects that are too broad. You can pare a big topic down to size by moving from the general to the specific. The general and abstract topic "Air Power," for example, may be successfully narrowed to the more concrete and specific "Combat Radius of the B-52." Here are the steps followed in limiting this subject:

- Air Power (much too abstract)
- Military Air Power (not much better)
- The Air Force (a beginning in the right direction)
- Strategic Air Command (a little more specific)
- The B-52 (something concrete)
- Combat Radius of the B-52 (a suitable topic)

Limit your subject in terms of your own interests and qualifications, your listeners' needs and demands, and the time allotted to your speech.

Choosing a Title

The title is a specific label given to the speech—an advertising slogan or catchword that catches the spirit of the speech and tantalizes the potential audience. Generally, the exact phrasing of the title is not decided until the speech has been built. At other times it may come to mind as you work on the speech. At still other times it may come early and guide your planning. An effective title should be relevant, provocative, and brief.

Listeners do not like to be misled. If the speech has to do with communication, then some reference to communication should be in the title. On the other hand, don't include words in the title merely to get attention if they have no relevance to the speech itself. "The Eleventh Commandment" is a relevant title for a speech that addresses the fact that the commandment of "Thou shall not get caught" has seemed to replace some of the other commandments. "A Pat on the Back, A Punch in the Mouth" is certainly a more provocative title than "How Positive and Negative Reinforcement Affects Our Children." "You Cannot *Not* Communicate" is briefer and more provocative than "The Impossibility of Failing to Communicate."

Although the preceding three titles are all rather catchy, sometimes the direct approach is very effective. Consider the very descriptive title given earlier, "Combat Radius of the B-52." A speech or lecture on effective listening might simply be titled "Effective Listening." Both of these titles are relevant, provocative (due to the subject matter itself), and brief.

Objectives

The purposes for speaking—informative, persuasive, entertaining—are important. But the general responses and specific responses you expect from the talks you give are also significant.

General Responses

The purposes of speaking suggest the general kinds of responses desired from the audience. An informative presentation seeks audience understanding. A persuasive presentation seeks a change in beliefs, attitudes, or behavior. An entertaining presentation seeks to divert, amuse, or, in some other way, cause listeners to enjoy themselves.

Specific Responses

In addition to the three broad purposes or aims, there are more specific purposes, sometimes referred to as goals or objectives, of speaking. An effective oral presentation has immediate and specific objectives stated in terms of what is expected from the listeners. These specific objectives fall within the broader purposes of information, persuasion, or entertainment. The objectives do not state what the speaker is to do. Rather they tell what the speaker wishes the audience to understand, believe, feel, do, or enjoy. The following examples illustrate the relationship between subjects, general purposes, and specific objectives:

1. Subject: From Iowa to the Air Force
   Purpose: To entertain
   Objective: For listeners to enjoy the humor of a young man from Iowa making the transition from an Iowa farm to the Air Force
2. Subject: You cannot *not* communicate
   Purpose: To inform
   Objective: For listeners to understand that we are constantly communicating verbally and nonverbally
3. Subject: Equality for all
   Purpose: To persuade
   Objective: For listeners to dedicate themselves anew to the principle of racial and social equality for all

Gathering Material

With the general purpose and specific objective in mind, you are ready to gather material on the subject. The source for this material should be your own experience or the experience of others gained through conversation, interviews, and written or observed material. You may often draw from all these sources in a single presentation.

Self

The first step in researching an oral presentation is the assembly of all the personal knowledge you have about the subject. A

self-inventory may suggest a tentative organization; but, even more important, it will point up gaps in knowledge where you need to do further research.

Others

The second step in the research process is to draw on the experience of others. People who are interested in the subject provide many ideas during the course of conversation. The most fruitful source, of course, is the expert. Experts help you clarify your thinking, provide facts, and suggest good sources for further research. Their suggestions for further sources can enable you to narrow your search without having to investigate a large bulk of material.

Library

The third step is library research. Modern libraries provide us with an abundance of sources—books, newspapers, popular magazines, scholarly journals, abstracts, subject files, microfilms. You must constantly be concerned with the accuracy and relevance of the material. Using material printed in 1950 to understand television today would probably lead to inaccurate, irrelevant conclusions.

Evaluating Material

The next step in the research process is to evaluate the material gathered. You will probably find that you have enough material for several presentations. If you haven't already begun to organize the presentation, you will want to do so. Next you will want to select the best kinds of support for the points you wish to make. Then you will want to prepare a good beginning and ending for the talk.

CHAPTER 2

ORGANIZING THE TALK

Clear organization is vital to effective speaking. The most prevalent weakness among speakers at all levels is the failure to organize material for the audience. Speakers have the responsibility to lead listeners mentally from where they are at the beginning of a talk to where they are supposed to be at the end. The message must be organized with the audience in mind; the organization should conform to the thinking processes and expectations of the listeners.

Each speech, lecture, and briefing needs an introduction, a body, and a conclusion. In most instances the introduction and conclusion should be prepared after the body of the talk, since the material in the body is a guide for preparing the introduction and conclusion.

The first consideration in planning the body is how to organize the main points, but organization of subpoints is also important. Arrangement of the main points and subpoints will help both the speaker and the audience remember the material—the speaker while speaking, and the audience while listening.

Most oral presentations, regardless of their length, can be divided into two to five main points. Five is about the maximum number of points from one talk that listeners can be expected to remember.

The most typical ways of organizing main points or subpoints of a talk are by the patterns: time, space, cause/effect, problem/solution, pro/con, or topic. Furthermore, as illustrated throughout this chapter, *certain strategies can be used with each pattern*. How does a speaker decide which patterns and strategies to use? The material will often organize more easily with one pattern and strategy than with another. Consider how various patterns and strategies can be used to organize the main points.

Time

Our vocabularies are filled with words that refer to time: now, tomorrow, yesterday, today, sooner, later, earlier, next (last) week (month, year, time). We work, play, sleep, and eat at certain times. Major events in our lives are organized by time: births, engagements, marriages, deaths. The time, or chronological pattern of organization, then, is a natural way of arranging events in the sequence or order in which they happened or in giving directions on the order to be followed in carrying out those events. This kind of organization is sometimes called *sequential organization*. Certain processes, procedures, or historical movements and developments can often be explained best with a time-sequence organizational pattern.

The medical technician discussing the mouth-to-mouth system of artificial respiration would probably use a time order for the main points: (1) preliminary steps in preparing the body—proper position, mouth open, tongue and jaw forward, (2) the mouth-to-mouth process, (3) caring for the patient once breathing resumes. Time order is also a logical approach for talks dealing with such subjects as "How to Pack a Parachute," "Development of the B-1 Bomber," or "How to Prepare a Speech." Furthermore, any talk on a subject with several phases lends itself well to the time pattern. For example, a talk with an objective for the audience to know that the common market was originally planned to develop in three phases might have as main points: (1) phase one, a customs union where nations agreed to reduce duties, (2) phase two, an economic union allowing laborers and goods to move freely across national borders, and (3) phase three, a political union with national representatives as members of a common parliament and using a common currency.

Of course, rather than looking forward in time from a given moment, the strategy might be to look backward from a point in time. In other words, the strategy might be to move from recent to earlier time rather than from early to late. Regardless of which strategy is used, the flow of the talk and the transitions from one point to the next should make the chronological relationship between main points clear to audience members.

Space

A spatial or geographical pattern is very effective in describing relationships. When using this pattern, the talk is developed according to some directional strategy such as east to west or north to south. For instance, if the speaker were describing the domino theory of Communist infiltration, the strategy would probably be to arrange the main points according to the geographical locations of various nations and how they would be affected by Communist infiltration within their geographical region.

With talks on certain objects, the strategy might be to arrange the main points from top to bottom or bottom to top. A fire extinguisher might be described from top to bottom, an organizational chart from the highest ranking individuals to the lowest ones in the organization, a library according to the services found on the first floor, then the second, and finally those on the third.

Sometimes, the strategy is to organize the talk from the center to the outside. For example, the control panel in an airplane might be discussed by describing first those often used instruments in the center, then by moving out toward the surrounding instruments which are used least often.

In all talks arranged spatially, each aspect or main point needs to be introduced according to the strategy used. Just as with a talk organized by time, the subject matter and the transitions should include elaboration and clarification of how the main points relate to one another. A simple listing of the various objects or places without elaboration as to how they are related may confuse the listeners.

Cause/Effect

A causal pattern of arrangement is used in a talk where one set of conditions is given as a cause for another set. In such talks, one of two basic strategies may be used to arrange main points. With a cause/effect strategy you begin with a given set of conditions and contend that these will produce or have already produced certain results or effects; with an effect/cause strategy you take a certain set of conditions as the effects and allege that they resulted from certain causes.

The cause/effect strategy might be used in a talk concerning the increasing number of women in the Air Force. The talk might first discuss the fact that women are now assuming more responsible leadership roles in the Air Force. One effect of women assuming such roles might be that women are joining the Air Force in increasing numbers.

The effect/cause strategy might be used in a talk on child abuse. The first point might explain the effects of child abuse upon the children themselves, the parents, and even on society. The second point might allege that the causes are that parents themselves were abused as children or that proper education on parenting was not received.

Whichever strategy is used, two cautions must be observed. (1) Beware of false causes. Just because one event or circumstance precedes another does not mean that the former causes the latter. Many persons assume that "first A happened, then B took place, so A must have caused B." (2) Beware of single causes. Few things result from a single cause. Many causes are more common with one playing on another until it is hard to disentangle them. Lack of safety features on automobiles is not the only cause of most highway accidents; but this cause, plus careless driving or unsafe highways, may account for many highway accidents.

Problem/Solution

This pattern, sometimes called the disease/remedy pattern or the need/satisfaction pattern, presents listeners with a problem and then proposes a way to solve it. With this pattern, you must show that a problem exists and then offer a corrective action that is (1) practical, (2) desirable, (3) capable of being put into action, and (4) able to relieve the problem. It must also be one that does not introduce new and worse evils of its own. For example, the issue of controlling nuclear weapons has long been debated. Those against control argue that erosion of national sovereignty from arms control is more dangerous than no control.

The problem/solution pattern is especially useful with briefings whose purpose is to provide listeners with information on which to base decisions. It can also be used effectively with persuasive speeches and teaching lectures where the speaker wants to present a need or a problem followed by a way or ways to satisfy the need or solve the problem.

There are different strategies that might be employed when using the problem/solution method. If the listeners are aware of the problem and the possible solutions, you will probably discuss the problem briefly, mention the possible solutions, then spend more time in showing why one solution is better than others. For instance, if the objective is for listeners to comprehend that solar energy is the best solution to the energy crisis, our main points might be: (1) The world is caught in the grip of an energy crisis. (2) Several solutions are possible. (3) Solar energy is the best long-term solution.

If the listeners are not aware or are only slightly aware of the problem or need, you may describe in detail the exact nature of the problem. Sometimes, when listeners become aware of the problem, the solution becomes evident and little time is needed to develop the solution in the lesson. At other times, you may need to spend time developing both the problem and the solution.

Still another strategy is to alternate or stagger portions of the problem with portions of the solution. For example, the cost of a project may be seen as one problem, workability another, time to do the projects as a third. Taking up each portion and, in turn, providing solutions to cost, workability, and time as you present these aspects of the problem may be more satisfying to your listeners than if you had discussed all of the problem and then its total solution. The problem/solution pattern is a good one for advocacy or persuasive briefings.

Pro/Con

The pro/con pattern, sometimes called the for/against pattern or advantages/disadvantages pattern, is similar to a problem/solution pattern in that the talk is usually planned so as to lead to a conclusion. A major difference, however, is that fairly even attention is usually directed toward both sides of an issue with a pro/con pattern.

There are various strategies to consider when using the pro/con pattern. One consideration is whether to present pro or con first. Another is whether to present both sides and let listeners draw their own conclusions or to present the material in such a way that listeners are led to accept the "school solution." For instance, with a talk on the effects of jogging, you must decide whether to present the advantages or disadvantages first. Then you must decide whether to let listeners make their own decision as to the advantages or disadvantages.

When deciding the specific strategy to use with the pro/con pattern and determining how much time to spend on each, the following guidelines may be helpful: (1) Giving both sides fairly even emphasis is most effective when the weight of evidence is clearly on the favored side. (2) Presenting both sides is most effective when listeners may be initially opposed to the school solution. (3) Presenting only the favored side is most effective when listeners already favor the school solution or conclusion. (4) Presenting the favored side last makes its acceptance more likely, especially if the other side is not shown in too favorable a light.

Topical

A topical division of the main points of a talk involves determining categories of the subject. This type of categorizing or classifying often springs directly from the subject itself. For instance, a talk about a typical college population might be divided into topical divisions of freshmen, sophomores, juniors, and seniors, with each class division serving as a main point. Housing might be discussed in terms of on-base and off-base housing. A talk on the MX intercontinental ballistic missile might be arranged according to the main points of warhead, guidance, and propulsion systems.

At times the material itself suggests certain strategies for ordering the main points. For instance, a talk on lesson planning would most likely begin with knowledge-level planning as the first main point since knowledge-level lessons are generally simpler to understand. Then the lesson would move on through the hierarchy to comprehension, application, analysis, synthesis, and, finally, evaluation levels. In other words your talk would follow a simple-to-complex strategy in organizing the "topics" or levels of lessons.

19

Other talks might follow strategies of known to unknown, general to specific, or specific to general arrangement of topical main points. There are many strategies for arranging topical main points. The important consideration, as with any pattern, is to give thought to the strategy of arrangement in order to help the listeners' understanding.

Combining Patterns

If a single pattern is used to organize the main points, your talks will make more sense. And as a speaker, you will be able to remember more readily what your main points are when you present the talk. Even more important, listeners will be able to follow the talk more easily and remember what you said if a single logical pattern of organization is used for the main points.

Although you may choose a certain organizational pattern for the main points, you may decide to use different patterns for subpoints. Consider the following tentative outline (fig. 1) of a talk with an objective or goal for listeners to know the importance of nonverbal factors of communication. Notice that the main points (1. Performance Factors, and 2. Nonperformance Factors) are arranged topically. The subpoints for main point 1 (upper, middle, and lower body) are organized spatially. A pro/con pattern is followed in discussing positive and negative effects from each body performance factor. The subpoints of main point 2 (objects, space, and time) are organized topically. Subpoints under 2a are organized by time. Subpoints under 2b are organized topically.

The important thing to remember is that *each set of main points or subpoints should follow a logical pattern of organization*. The tentative outline reflects this fact. Of course, it may be that none of the formal patterns of organization discussed in this chapter adequately fits your content. For instance, with a speech to entertain, you might simply string together a group of interesting or humorous incidents that would hold the audience's attention. But whatever the case, you must strive to organize your talk

---

NONVERBAL COMMUNICATION

1. Performance Factors

    a. Upper Body (head and face)

        (1) Positive Effects
        (2) Negative Effects

    b. Middle Body (arms, hands, torso)

        (1) Positive Effects
        (2) Negative Effects

    c. Lower Body (hips, legs, feet)

        (1) Positive Effects
        (2) Negative Effects

2. Nonperformance Factors

    a. Objects

        (1) Present
        (2) Past

    b. Space

        (1) Personal
        (2) Constructed

    c. Time

Figure 1

in a way that will help you present the information to your listeners in the most meaningful fashion. As you construct a tentative outline, you must do so with your listeners' needs in mind. Quite often, the experienced speaker revises the outline three or four times before being satisfied and finally putting it into final form for the talk.

Now that You Have Organized

The organization patterns and strategies you choose provide structure to the body of your talk. But structure without content is not enough. Interesting and effective supporting material is needed. To use an anatomical analogy, the organization provides the skeleton and the supporting material supplies the flesh for the body of the talk. The next chapter discusses how to choose effective visual and verbal support for the talk. The following chapter suggests how to begin and end various kinds of talks. The final chapter tells how to present talks.

CHAPTER 3

SUPPORTING THE TALK

Most listeners find it difficult to understand unsupported ideas or assertions. Suppose, for instance, you decide to speak on "How to Organize a Talk." You tell your listeners that they can organize a talk according to one of several possible patterns of presentation. You then tell them that the most common patterns are: time, space, cause/effect, problem/solution, pro/con, and

topic. Most likely you will not have provided enough information for your listeners to actually use these patterns of organization. You will need to go on and explain each of these patterns as has been done in the preceding chapter.

Factors to Consider

Consider all factors when choosing support. The subject of your talk, the type of talk (briefing, lecture, or speech), and the composition of your audience will help you determine the amount and kinds of support to use.

Briefing

For a briefing, support is generally limited to factual data carefully selected to accomplish the "need to know." The requirement for brevity dictates that you not use extraneous or "nice to know" support. Visual aids are often used to save time and achieve accuracy. Humor is seldom used. If the purpose of the briefing is persuasive, use logic rather than emotion to persuade.

Teaching Lecture

Factual material is also important in the teaching lecture, although there may be a need to use support that also appeals strongly to the emotions. Humor and other attention-commanding materials are common throughout the lecture. Visual aids are often used, not only to save time and improve accuracy but also to clarify ideas.

Speech

Informative speeches use much the same support as teaching lectures. Entertaining speeches rely heavily on humor and other attention-getting support. Persuasive speeches are characterized by more appeal to emotions or motives than any other kind of talk you will give. Appeal to such motives as fear, curiosity, loyalty, adventure, pride, and sympathy is common in persuasion. The distinction between logical and emotional support, however, is in content rather than form. Any type of verbal and visual support mentioned in this chapter may be primarily logical or emotional. *But just because support appeals to the emotions does not mean it has to be illogical.*

Logical Thinking

Both verbal and visual support, whether used primarily for emotional or logical appeals, should be backed by logical thinking. Here are some problems that commonly affect logical thinking of persons preparing talks.

Slanted Reasoning

Slanted reasoning occurs when a speaker makes invalid inferences or reaches false conclusions due to faulty reasoning. Several common types of slanted reasoning follow:

1. The hasty generalization happens when a speaker judges a whole class of objects from an insufficient sample. The person who meets two persons from Alabama and dislikes them, and based on a sample of two, concludes that all people from Alabama are unlikable is guilty of making a hasty generalization.

2. The faulty dilemma stems from the fact that although some objects or qualities can be divided into discrete categories, most cannot. Deeds that are not evil are not necessarily good. A cup of coffee may be neither hot nor cold; it may be lukewarm.

3. The faulty analogy happens when a speaker assumes that two things alike in some way or ways are alike in all ways. The human body and an automobile engine are alike in many respects: both must operate within certain temperature limits, both last

longer if cared for, both consume fuel. But you would not argue that since adding tetraethyl lead to gasoline makes an automobile engine run better, people should put tetraethyl lead in their coffee.

4. Stacking the evidence occurs when speakers lift out of context only the support that fits their talk while ignoring equally important material that is detrimental to points they are trying to make.

5. Faulty causal reasoning is seen when a speaker reasons that if A is present, B occurs; further if A is absent, B does not occur; therefore, the speaker reasons that A causes B. Of course it could be that B causes A, or perhaps both are caused by a third ingredient, C.

Irrational Appeals

Irrational appeals depend upon blind transfer of feelings from one thing to another without logical thought. Consider the following examples of irrational appeal.

1. Name calling refers to putting people or things in a bad light by calling them uncomplimentary names such as fatso, warmonger, Seward's Icebox.

2. Glittering generalities are apparent when speakers wrap their ideas in good, golden, glittering words such as *peace, culture, equality,* and *flag*.

3. Bandwagon appeal operates on the principle that "everyone else is doing it so you should too." Some speakers use the bandwagon appeal to promote the feeling that listeners would be presumptuous to judge for themselves something that the group accepts.

4. "Plain folks" strategy is used when speakers attempt to identify with the simple (and presumably desired) things of life. A speaker who says in front of a farm audience, "I know how you feel, I was born and raised on a farm, and I want to keep the big city politicians' hands off your property tax money," is using plain-folks strategy. Identifying with your audience is a sound practice, but identification alone is not rational support.

5. Prestige or transfer is used by those who drop names or use other strategies to appear important. They believe that simply associating themselves with certain personalities will cause listeners to associate desired traits of those personalities with them as the speakers.

Verbal Support

Verbal support is used either to clarify the points you wish to make or to prove your assertions. Definitions, examples, and comparisons are used primarily for clarification. Statistics and testimony of experts can be used either for clarification or proof. Humor can be used with any of the preceding five types of verbal support and will be treated separately in this chapter.

Definitions

Definitions are often needed to clarify or explain the meaning of a term, concept, or principle. But like so many words, definition can mean different things and can function in different ways.

In some talks you may need to use words that are technical, complex, or strange to your listeners. With increasing specialization in the Air Force in both theoretical and applied subjects, the development of new words or terms races ahead of dictionaries. Words such as pneudraulics (military aircraft brake systems), taxonomy (scientific classification), détente (military strategy) or groupthink (a problem of groups) might require literal definitions or restatement in simpler language.

At other times there is a need to define words that are frequently loosely employed. Some words simply have different meanings for different people. Words such as democracy, equal rights, security needs, and loyalty can usually be defined easily. For instance, disseminate can be defined very simply as "spread widely." Sometimes a speaker may seek novel and memorable ways to define such terms. Pragmatism might be defined as "a fancy word to mean that the proof of the pudding is in the eating.'' Sometimes it takes a little longer to fully define what is meant by a certain term. A former POW might define the sacrifice of one prisoner for another:

> When you see an American prisoner giving up his meager ration of fish, just so another American who is sick can have a little more to eat, that is sacrifice. Because when you don't have anything, and you give it up, or you have very little and you give it up, then you're hurting yourself, and that is true sacrifice. That's what I saw in the prison camp.

Definitions should also be used to explain the meaning of acronyms—words or other combinations of letters formed from the initial letter of each of the successive parts of a compound term. In the preceding paragraph, with some audiences, it might have been necessary to explain that POW stands for prisoner of war. If you were discussing PME at AU, you might have to explain that PME at AU means professional military education that is taught at Air University. Furthermore, you might go on to mention that PME includes AWC, ACSC, SOS, and SNCOA— that is, Air War College, Air Command and Staff College, Squadron Officer School, and the Senior Noncommissioned Officer Academy.

Finally, at times an entire talk may be needed to define or otherwise introduce students to a new concept or principle— for example, a speaker discussing the concept of communication as transaction. Perhaps an entire lecture would be needed to explain that the transactional approach means to consider the total communication process and the interaction of the various parts of the process on each other. Other forms of support material such as examples and comparisons would be needed to fully define what was meant.

Examples

Any time other persons ask you to "give a for instance," they are asking for an example to clarify the point you are trying to make. Sometimes the examples may be reasonably long. The parables of Jesus, the stories of Homer, Aesop's *Fables*, and many of the stories that appeared in the speeches of Abraham Lincoln are detailed examples.

At other times a short example is sufficient. In some cases short examples are similar to definitions. The earlier definition of *sacrifice* given by the former POW might be considered a short example. The fact that some support materials might be classed either as definitions or examples should not be a major concern to you. As a speaker, you are more interested in *using* effective support material than in classifying it.

Often short examples can be clustered together in order to help listeners gain a more complete understanding of the point. In a talk on barriers to effective communication, a speaker might cluster examples of spoonerisms: "Is the bean dizzy?" ("Is the dean busy?"); "I'll have a coff of cuppee" ("I'll have a cup of coffee"); "A half-warmed fish within us" ("A half-formed wish within us").

You should ask yourself several questions about examples you plan to use:

- Do they accurately represent the point?
- Will listeners clearly understand their meaning?
- Do they fit the content? (Avoid those that may confuse.)
- Will humorous ones add or detract from the lesson? (Some guidelines for using humor are presented later in this chapter.)
- Do they come from personal experience or can other examples be personalized in such a way as to seem real?
- Can anything be gained from clustering more than three or four examples? Usually not.
- Do long ones take too much time? (At times, attention-getting value of long examples may justify their use.)
- Are they interesting?

The appropriate answers to these questions should be obvious.

Comparisons

Description often becomes more graphic when we place an unknown or little understood item beside a similar but better known item. You might want to compare things that are unlike or things that are very much alike.

Metaphors such as Winston Churchill's "iron curtain" or similies (using the words "like" or "as" such as Robert Burns's "My love is like a red, red rose" or saying "strong as an ox") are comparisons of things that are unlike in most ways. Speakers may compare unlike things. For instance, one might say, "The flow of knowledge is like the relentless and uncompromising flow of a river after the spring thaw as it imposes on us the requirement that we not only adjust to, but anticipate, the future." Or a speaker might show that being a member of a branch in an Air Force organization is like living in a family where we have intimate contact with each other. The analogy or comparison might be carried further by pointing out that in a branch, as in a family, members can protect one another, help one another, and irritate each other.

Although analogies that compare dissimilar things serve as an excellent means of clarification, they have limited utility as proof. If you wish to support an assertion, you must compare similar things. Comparison of Soviet air power with US air power or the relationship between the mayor and city council with the relationship between the base commander and his staff are like comparisons. Arguing that a longer orientation session for students in a certain NCO academy would improve academic performance because it did at another NCO academy would be comparing like phenomena—in this case, two NCO academies.

Contrast is a special form of comparison. For instance, showing how Air Force training differs from Army training or how today's standard of living differs from that of a generation ago clarifies and explains a point by showing contrast or differences.

Obviously, comparisons may be very brief such as those given here or they may be quite long. You need to decide what will work best in a given situation. But whether long or short, comparisons are a valuable and generally underused method of verbal support.

Testimony

Words and thoughts of others are particularly useful when you wish to add strong proof support for assertions or points that you make. No one is expected to be an expert on all subjects; speakers often must rely on what others have said. At times testimony of others is used simply to clarify or explain an idea; often it is intended to provide proof for a claim.

If you are presenting a talk on managerial effectiveness in an organization, one of your main points might be the importance of effective downward communication. In other words, you want to stress how important it is for supervisors to keep their subordinates informed. You might quote from an *Air Force Policy Letter for Commanders*, which comes from the Office of the Secretary of the Air Force. It says, "Commanders and supervisors have an increased responsibility to keep Air Force military and civilian members informed." You might also report the findings from a study by the International Association of Business Communicators which show that "face-to-face communication, including group meetings and one-on-one dialogue," proved the most effective means of communicating with employees. Sometimes, you will want to use direct quotations as we have done here. At other times you will paraphrase what another has said. Whatever the case, there are two tests of testimony: (1) Are the sources competent—do they know what they are talking about? and (2) Can they be trusted—are they free from bias? Other considerations are: Is the testimony relevant, clear, and interesting? Are the quotations longer than necessary?

Statistics

Statistics are probably the most misused and misunderstood type of verbal support. When properly collected and wisely used, statistics can help speakers clarify their ideas. Statistics are also the most powerful proof support we can use. However, not all figures are statistics, some are simply numbers. Statistics show relationships, largeness or smallness, increases or decreases, or summarize large collections of facts or data. When you choose statistics, there are some questions to ask.

1. Are the statistics recent? Figures concerning the cost of living in 1960 would have limited usefulness for today's family planning its budget. When selecting statistics to use, be on guard if no date is given or if the statistics are outdated.

2. Do the statistics indicate what they purport to? A single test score may not be a true measure of a student's ability. The number of planes may not indicate the strength of the Air Force.

3. Do the statistics cover a long enough time or enough samples to be reliable? The results of how one class responded to a new curriculum change would be less meaningful than how three or four classes responded to the change.

4. If the statistics are drawn from a sample, does the sample accurately represent the group to which we are generalizing? Public opinion surveys and experimental researchers are generally sensitive to the importance of obtaining a representative sample. Speakers also need to be sensitive to this need.

5. When statistics report differences, are the differences significant? Minor variations can often be attributed to chance. In other words, if you were to collect your statistics again, the results might differ.

6. When comparing things, are the units of measure compared the same? Failure in one course might have a different meaning than failure in another. If more students fail one course than another, you cannot necessarily conclude that the content of one course is more difficult. Perhaps the grading scale rather than the content was more difficult.

7. Do the statistics come from a good, reliable source? And is the source clearly indicated? It is more effective to state the source of the information than to say "recent surveys show."

8. Are the statistics presented to their best advantage to aid listener understanding? Could visual aids be used to present the statistics in graphic or tabular form for easier understanding? Have figures been rounded off where possible? Listeners are more likely to remember "nearly $45,000" than "$44,871.24." Are the number of statistics limited so that listeners are not overwhelmed by them? Could the significance of statistics be made more clear with meaningful comparisons? To say that World War

II cost the United States $200 billion would not be as clearly perceived as if the figures were converted to today's dollars or if they were compared to the cost of a war today using a standard measure.

Humor

Most listeners admire a speaker who can use humor effectively. Yet few speakers are able to do so. Moreover, when humor is used, it is generally only at the beginning to gain audience attention. Humor can be used with good results in the body of a talk.

There are two reasons to use humor in the body of a talk. One is to recapture the attention of the audience. The attention span of most people is only a few minutes; so unless the material is terribly engaging, a speaker can recall instances when an audience's attention wandered. Humor regains attention. The second reason to use humor in the body of a talk is to emphasize an important point. Although a story or anecdote is seldom real proof, it may reinforce your audience's ability to remember the point.

Humor must be used properly if it is to be effective. There are six essentials to using humor.

1. Know the item thoroughly. We have all heard speakers stumble through a potentially humorous item or make it through in fine shape only to forget the punch line. But if speakers know the story and have told it before, they will be able to tell it again and know the kind of response to expect. It is generally a good rule for speakers not to use a story or humorous item of any kind in a speech unless they have told it several times in informal situations so they can both practice and gauge the reactions of others.

2. Don't use inappropriate humor. Some speakers consider off-color stories or ethnic humor as a cheap way to get a laugh from an audience. But even people who laugh at such stories in private often lose respect for the speaker who uses them in public.

Deciding if a joke is inappropriate is not always easy. If there is doubt, the story probably isn't appropriate.

3. Vitalize humor. Stories should be personalized so they are believable, so they sound as if they really happened. Rather than talk about "this guy I heard about," or "this truck driver," the speaker should give the characters in the stories names. Successful raconteurs and speakers nearly always vitalize their humor.

4. Don't laugh before the audience laughs. Some comedians get away with laughing first, but good speakers never laugh before the audience. If a speaker fails to get the story across, laughing alone on a platform is disaster. If the joke fails, the speaker is best advised to leave it and go on.

5. Capitalize on the unexpected. One of the primary elements of humor is that people laugh when they are surprised. A few years ago, streaking was a fad on college campuses. Most first-hand observers laughed when confronted by a streaker. Some of the laughter was no doubt due to embarrassment; most of it was due to the element of surprise. The following are all types of humor that depend on the unexpected: quips (of course, men aren't what they used to be—they used to be boys), puns (try our bread, we knead the dough), exaggeration (the heat was so terrific last week that I saw a hound dog chasing a rabbit; they were both walking), understatement (if at first you don't succeed, well, so much for skydiving).

6. See humor in the situation. The best opportunity for adding humor may come in those minutes just before you speak. It may come from things said by those preceding you on the program. It may come from malfunction of your visual aids, getting tangled up in the microphone cord, or from a person sneezing in your audience. And although much of this situational humor may not directly support the point you are making, it can nevertheless help win your audience.

Being witty and humorous is not easy. It helps to have an agile and sophisticated mind—one that adapts skillfully to the audience. Yet many more speakers could use humor effectively if they were willing to try and willing to practice.

Visual Support

Verbal support is certainly at the heart of any good talk, but visual aids can function to dramatize, amplify, or clarify the points you are trying to get across to your audience. AU–1, volume 8, *Easy Visual Aids*, emphasizes easy to construct and inexpensive visual aids for various kinds of speaking situations. However, in this book the emphasis is solely on how to *use* visual aids.

Suggestions

Some basic suggestions apply to visual aids that might be used with any type of talk you give.

1. Use only materials that are relevant. Avoid using materials solely for aesthetic or interest value. Certainly, visual materials should be interesting, but the primary purpose of any visual aid is to portray or support an idea graphically for your listeners. Irrelevant materials distract from the idea you are presenting.

2. Use visual materials that are large enough to be seen by all the audience. Nothing is so disturbing as to be seated in the back of the room unable to see the visual aids. In preparing for your talk, display the visual aids, then move yourself to the location of your most distant listener. If you can't readily see the material, consider replacing it with something more appropriate.

3. Use visual materials only at the proper time. Do not expose the visual material until the proper point in the talk. Clearly mark your notes or outline so you will know when to use each piece of visual support. Materials that are visible too soon or that remain in view after the point has been made distract from and interrupt the continuity of the talk. You may want to use the "striptease" or buildup method for revealing a series of points. Don't list ten main points for the audience and then discuss each one. Instead, uncover the points one at a time to keep the audience's attention focused.

4. Keep visual materials as simple and as clear as possible. Emphasize only the most important information. Omit unnecessary details. A series of simple charts is preferable to a single complicated one.

5. Talk to the audience, not to the visual aid. If you are explaining a chart, look at your audience as much as possible. By the time you make your talk, you should be so familiar with your visual aids that it will be unnecessary for you to look at them closely. When possible, paraphrase the visual material instead of reading it, or pause and let the audience read it silently.

6. Place visual aids away from obstructions. Don't allow other projects or persons—including yourself—to obstruct the view of your audience. You decided to use visual materials to support and clarify your talk. Don't hinder their effectiveness by obstructing the audience's view.

7. If you plan to use equipment such as an overhead projector, a slide projector, or a film projector, make certain beforehand that you know how to use the equipment and that it is set up and ready to go. Also, know whether or not you have a spare bulb, how to change it, or how to improvise and do without the equipment. In other words, be ready for any contingencies that may develop. Many potentially sound presentations fail because the speaker fails to plan for equipment that malfunctions.

8. When using flipcharts, consider flipping from back to front rather than from front to back. There are at least three advantages. First, flipping back to front is easier—try it if you don't think so. Second, flipping from back to front can be done from the side of the charts rather than from the front—between the charts and the audience—as you generally have to do when flipping from front to back. Third, if the paper you use for the charts is relatively thin, the back to front procedure prevents your audience from reading through the paper to a chart you haven't yet discussed.

9. Finally, before you construct a visual aid, ask yourself if the effort and expense required to prepare or procure the aid are justified and add significantly to the overall value of the talk. If not, forget it. Often the time spent preparing visual aids could be better spent preparing and practicing the talk.

Using a Chalkboard

If you use a chalkboard, consider the following additional suggestions:

1. Pare the chalk to desired thickness so that the lines you draw are ¼ to ⅜ inches wide. Have spare pieces of chalk ready for use.

2. Use a No. 2 soft pencil and yardstick to make erasable guidelines on the board before your audience enters the room. Later when writing on the board during your talk you can ensure straight and even lettering by following lines invisible to your audience.

3. Cramping your letters and diagrams cramps your speaking. To be seen easily at 30 feet, letters should be about three inches high.

4. Avoid using the bottom half of the board if you are speaking from the same floor level as your audience since some listeners may be unable to see.

5. Determine where glare on the board is a distraction. Before the audience enters the room adjust window shades or avoid these areas of the board.

6. If the room is equipped with a magnetic chalkboard, or if some other metal surface such as a file cabinet is nearby, consider preconstructed visual aids with magnets glued to the back. Reusable magnetic material one-inch wide can be purchased in long lengths and cut easily to the desired length. Two magnets one-inch square will support one square foot of lightweight illustration board.

After You Have Your Support

By this time you have considered the unique factors of your talk. You have decided whether to present a briefing, a lecture, or some type of speech. You have considered your audience, your subject, your objectives and have gathered your material.

You have organized the body of the talk and have selected the kinds of verbal and visual support you will use with careful thought toward being logical in your use of support. Two important ingredients must be supplied before you are ready to work on presenting your talk. You need to plan a good introduction and a good conclusion.

CHAPTER 4

BEGINNING AND ENDING THE TALK

Once you have organized and supported the body of the talk with appropriate verbal and visual materials, you must decide how to begin and end. For many persons, beginning (or providing an introduction to the body of the talk) and ending (providing a conclusion) is most troublesome. Introductions and conclusions should fit the audience, the speaker, and the type of talk you are giving.

Briefing

Since briefings are to be brief, lengthy introductions and conclusions are inappropriate.

Introduction

Your listeners need and want to know about your subject; therefore, you will not need to spend time getting their attention. If, as often happens, another speaker introduces you and your subject, you need only give a quick overview of the subject and proceed immediately to the main points. Your listeners' familiarity with the subject will determine the length of the overview. In most cases simply mentioning the main points is sufficient. If you are not introduced, you might simply say, "Good morning, I'm _____ briefing on _____."

Conclusion

This part of a briefing should be short but positive. If your briefing is to stop with a listing of possible solutions or courses of action, a brief listing or summary of your points can give a sense of completion. If your briefing ends with a conclusion, as in a staff study report, you may end with a brief, clear restatement of the possible solution you judge best. No new material or commentary should be presented here. Or you may conclude by making a short statement recommending the action that would put your solution into effect.

Although many briefings are subject to interruption for questions from listeners, many times a good concluding sentence might be: "Ladies and Gentlemen, are there any (further) questions?" If a question period is not to follow, or once the questions have ended, you might simply say, "Ladies and Gentlemen, that concludes my briefing." At other times, the ranking person listening to the briefing may conclude the question period for you by declaring, "We have no further questions."

Teaching Lecture

Introductions and conclusions to teaching lectures are very important. Much care should be given to their development and use.

Introduction

The introduction to a teaching lecture should serve several purposes: to establish a common ground between the instructor and students, to capture and hold attention, to outline the lecture and relate it to the overall course, to point out benefits to the students, and to lead the students into the lecture content. Although humor may be appropriate, the introduction should be free of irrelevant stories, jokes, or incidents that distract from the lesson objective, and it should not contain long or apologetic remarks that are likely to dampen student interest in the lesson. Educators often speak of three necessary elements in the introduction of a lecture: gain attention, motivate, and provide an overview of material to be covered in the lecture.

Attention. To gain attention, the instructor may tell a story that relates to the subject and provides a background for the lecture. Another approach may be to make an unexpected or surprising statement or ask a question that relates the lecture to group needs. A rhetorical question (Have you ever . . . ? or, Can you imagine . . . ?) might be effective. At other times, nothing more than a clear indication that the lecture has begun is sufficient. In all instances, the primary concern is to focus student attention on the subject. Later in this chapter, general suggestions for getting audience attention are discussed.

Motivation. You should use the introduction to discuss specific reasons why the students need to learn whatever you want them to learn. In this motivational discussion, you should make a personal appeal to students and reinforce their desire to learn. The appeal may relate the learning to career advancement, financial gain, service to the community, use at home, or to some other need, but in every instance, you should cite a specific application for student learning experiences. In many cases, the need for this lecture as a foundation for future lessons is strong motivation. This motivational appeal should continue throughout the lecture. If you briefly mention student needs only in the introduction, you are square-filling, not motivating.

Overview. For most instructional methods, the introduction should provide an overview of what is to be covered during the class period. A clear, concise presentation of the objective and key ideas serves as a road map for the learning route. Effective visual aids can be helpful at this point. A clear overview can contribute greatly to a lecture by removing doubts in the minds of the learners about where the lesson is going and how they are going to get there. Students can be told what will be covered or left out and why. They can be informed about how the ideas have been organized. Research shows that students understand better and retain more when they know what to expect. The purpose of the overview is to prepare students to listen to the body of the lecture.

Conclusion

The conclusion of a lecture may stick with the students longer than anything else said. For this reason you should give much care to its preparation. The conclusion of most lectures should accomplish three things: summarize, remotivate, and provide closure.

Final Summary. Mini- or interim summaries may be appropriate at various places in a lecture—for example, after each main point has been made. But final summaries come after all main points of the lecture have been made. An effective final summary retraces the important elements discussed in the body. As the term suggests, a final summary reviews the main points of the lecture in a concise manner. By reviewing the main points, it can aid students' retention of information and give them a chance to fill in missing information in their notes.

Remotivation. The purpose of the remotivation is to instill in students a desire to retain and use what they have learned. Effective instructors provide motivation throughout the lecture. But the remotivation step is the instructor's last chance to let students know why the information presented in the lecture is so important to the student as an individual. Perhaps it is important because it provides the groundwork for future lessons or because it will help them do their jobs more effectively. But whatever the reasons given, they should be ones that appeal directly to the students and show the importance to them of what was learned.

Closure. For many instructors the closure presents a difficult challenge. The students need to be released from listening. Sometimes instructors at a loss on how to close say, "Well that's about all I have to say," or "I guess I don't have anything else." This type of closure is not very satisfying. There are much more effective ways of closing. Sometimes vocal inflection can signal that the lecture is ending. Quotations, stories, or humorous incidents can also provide effective closure. Sometimes when the lecture is to be followed by other lessons in the same block of instruction, you might say something such as "Next time, then, we will continue with our discussion of _____. Between now and then if you have any questions, come to my office and I'll see if I can answer them for you."

Speech

All speeches need introductions and conclusions. But the types of introductions and conclusions needed may differ greatly from speech to speech.

Introduction

For many speeches you will most likely want to use the same three steps of attention, motivation, and overview that you would use for a teaching lecture. There are times, however, when such an introduction might not be appropriate.

At times an attention step may not be needed. A well-known general addressing students at an Air Force school, a war hero talking to a local veterans organization, a prominent family counselor speaking to a group of married couples who chose to attend the talk all have their audiences' attention at the beginning. Still, attention of the audiences is not something that can be taken for granted.

One of America's better known ministers confides that he spends more time on what he refers to as his opening "hook" than any other part of the talk. He explains that if he can hook the audiences' attention at the beginning, he then only needs to keep their attention. Although keeping attention is not always an easy task, it is not as difficult as initially gaining the attention. This minister will sometimes devote three to five minutes of a twenty-minute talk to his "hook" or attention step. At times he uses humor; at times an engaging human interest story or example, but in all cases he sets the stage for the rest of his talk by using attention-getting material that relates directly to the body of his talk.

If you can't decide whether or not you need an attention step in your speech, then you probably do. Most talks will be improved with the addition of an effective attention step.

Although some sort of attention device is usually needed in a speech, at times a motivation step may be unnecessary. For instance, if your listeners are highly motivated to listen, then a motivation step establishing their need to listen would be out of place or redundant at best.

A short time ago, a world-class runner was conducting a clinic on running. Each participant had paid a substantial fee to attend. This well-known runner did not need to tell the audience why it was important for them to listen. The commitment to listen was already present. The listeners would not have paid their money to listen if they had not believed that this expert had some valuable information for them. Much like the military briefer, the speaker was able to launch immediately into the body of the speech and present hints and techniques helpful to runners.

Every good speaker, of course, attempts to motivate listeners throughout the speech. No matter how much credibility you have on the subject or how willing your audience is to listen to you,

46

you have a responsibility to provide continuing motivation for them to listen throughout the talk.

The overview step needed in most teaching lectures is unnecessary in many speeches. In fact, with speeches to persuade it may be advantageous if you do not preview what is to follow—especially if the audience does not initially share your point of view. If speakers tell their audiences what they want to persuade them to believe or do, they may turn audiences against them before they even begin. Also, the material in some speeches—such as some speeches to entertain—may not lend itself to an overview. Generally, in an informative speech, some type of overview is helpful, even if the overview consists only of mentioning the main points or telling them what you are going to tell them. The best advice is to consider the audience, occasion, and objectives of your speech, then decide if an overview is appropriate.

Conclusion

In some speeches you may choose to use the same three steps of summary, remotivation, and closure appropriate for teaching lectures. As with the introduction, however, the speaking situation will help determine what kind of conclusion is best.

Most speeches will not require an extensive conclusion. With informative speeches you may want to summarize briefly the main points you covered. With persuasive speeches, your conclusion may be a motivating statement of what you want your listeners to believe or how you want them to act. With an entertaining speech there may be little to actually summarize or motivate about.

All kinds of speeches, however, need some type of closure to provide completeness. Most speakers seem to give little thought to how to conclude. You can be assured that the time you spend attending to this detail will be time well spent since it is the last impression that the audience often carries with them when you have finished.

47

Suggestions for Gaining Attention

Although different types of talks require different kinds of introductions, some general suggestions may be helpful. Many of the following suggestions will be useful for gaining attention in lectures and speeches. Some of them are definitely not appropriate for military briefings. You will have to decide which ones apply to the talk you are giving.

Question

You will want your audience to respond in one of two ways. If you begin with a question—"What has been the most significant event in your life?''—you will not expect an audible answer, for the question is a rhetorical one. But you do expect your audience to think of an answer. The other type of question is one in which you expect an answer. The purpose is to get a unified audience reaction. "Do you want to keep on paying high taxes?" The politician using this question may want the audience to respond in unison, "No!"

Questions are easy to design. Good questions are a little more difficult. "Have you ever wondered how many people drive Chevrolets?" is not a good question. Many people in your audience reply mentally, "No, and I don't care." A question such as "Would you like to earn a million dollars next week?" is also ineffective since it is pretty far from reality. You should also avoid confusing questions: "How much fuel was used by the US Air Force, the air forces of other Western nations, and all commercial airlines from these countries during the past five years?"; and questions that may embarrass: "How many of you are deeply in debt?" Good questions are clear and direct and invite involvement from the audience: "What job do you want in 5 years?" "If you had one wish, what would it be?"

Quotation

Usually without looking too hard, you can find someone both authoritative and popular who is enthusiastic and supports your point of view. Practically every library has a copy of Bartlett's *Familiar Quotations*. Or if you speak often, you may wish to invest in one of the many specialized paperback versions on the market. There are quotation books especially for teachers, salesmen, speakers, ministers, and others. Also, if you keep your eyes open, you will come across quotations in your day-to-day reading that you can use later on. Make it a practice to write them down and file them away for future use. When you do use a quotation to open a talk, remember to keep it brief and understandable. You want to gain the audience's attention, not lose it.

Joke

Many speakers would be well advised not to open with a joke. When you buy a joke book from the local bookstore or check one out from the library, you find nothing but old gags about in-laws, drunks, and talking horses. A comedian or skilled raconteur can make the jokes funny with appropriate lead-in lines, timing, and putting the story into a believable context.

If you do wish to use a joke or humorous story, read again the suggestions for using humor given in the previous chapter. Especially attend to the suggestion to tell the story several times before using it in the talk so that you know it well and know the kind of response to expect. Also remember to make sure the story adds rather than detracts from your talk by making certain it is relevant, humorous, and not offensive to your audience. Many speakers have put themselves at serious disadvantage at the beginning of their talk by failing to consider these things.

Startling Statement

"Tonight more people will watch a typical situation comedy on TV than have seen all of the stage performances of all of Shakespeare's plays in the last 400 years." (This happens to be a true statement.) "When I was 14 years old I fell in love with a woman 37 feet tall." This statement would be a novel way to start a talk about a 37-foot statue in one's hometown. Remember to make your statement not only startling, but relevant.

Gimmick

Novelty openings are distinctive, creative, and usually visual. A CMSgt opened his talk on creative visual aids by quickly drawing an attractive picture on the chalkboard and saying, "When we have completed this two-hour block of instruction, I guarantee that you will be able to draw this well." Then he went on to explain that he had predrawn the picture on the board with a pencil and traced it with chalk, and in fact he was going to show the audience how to use techniques like this to improve their use of visual aids.

Gimmicks such as tearing a five-dollar bill in half, blowing a loud whistle, or taking off one's coat and hurling it across the room may be illegal, dangerous, or simply not relevant. Think through any gimmick that you plan to use. Try it on a few friends first to get their reaction. Then make certain it is legal, safe, and relevant to your talk.

Common Ground

A speaker establishes common ground by mentioning a common interest relevant to the subject at hand. This technique should be distinguished from the "plain-folks" appeal mentioned in the previous chapter. Unlike the politician who reminds his audience that he too was born and raised on a farm—a claim that may be true but is probably unrelated to his topic—common ground is established on a point relevant to the talk. And it is sincere. When visiting a university at which he once was a student, a professor might begin: "It is a real pleasure to be in Iowa City, to visit again this university where I received two degrees, and to have the opportunity to renew so many happy and precious friendships. It was here that many of my ideas about communication theory and public speaking were formed."

Reference

Many times you can gain the audience's attention simply by referring to the occasion, significance of the subject, special interest of the audience, or what a previous speaker has said.

Occasion. Several years ago, during our country's bicentennial, a speaker began: "We are assembled to celebrate the two-hundredth birthday of the United States." A speech commemorating the world's first night flight in Montgomery, Alabama, began: "Today we are gathered on a very historic spot. It was here at the Wright Flying School that the first successful night flight was completed."

Subject. The method of referring to the subject is closely related to the earlier comments concerning the motivation step appropriate for the lecture. The method is simple. Develop the attention around the implied theme: My subject is important to you now. In other words, tell the listeners why they should listen to you. This approach is most successful when you do not actually tell the listeners why the subject is important, since actually telling them often results in a colorless, trite statement. You simply think of the two or three reasons why the subject is significant, then state and amplify them until the audience reacts favorably. A slight variation is to start something like this: "I am not afraid that you will underestimate the importance of what I have to say today, for the subject of _____ concerns everybody."

Special Interests. A speaker addressing a local Lions Club known for its support of the Blue-Gray football game each year to raise money for the eye bank program might start: "The Blue-Gray football game is enjoyed annually through nationwide TV. But how many of its viewers know that it is more than a game with some of this country's finest professional prospects? All of us in this room know that this game helps people see."

Previous Speaker. When several speakers appear on one occasion, an alert speaker can often shape an opening based on what someone else has already said. This means is particularly effective since the reference is fresh in the listeners' minds and gives a sense of spontaneity to the talk. If you use this approach you can either explain how your subject fits with the previous talk or show a plausible relation between the two. For example: "Sergeant Henry just told you how important it is to use effective support in your talks. I am going to speak on something even more basic. I want to suggest how important it is to provide a good organizational framework in which to use the kinds of support Sergeant Henry talked about.''

Transitions and Interim Summaries

Transitions and interim summaries can be used to help the audience understand the continuity of thought and focus on main ideas.

Transitions

Transitions are statements used by the speaker to move from the introduction to the body of the talk, between main points, between subpoints within each main point, and from the body to the conclusion of the talk. Transitions signal to the audience that you are progressing to a new point, but they are also important in maintaining the continuity of the information being given. Consider this transition:

> We have discussed the precedents for a mandatory physical fitness program in the military. Next we will consider the benefits of such a program.

This transition indicates a change in direction, but it does not indicate the reason for or importance of the change.

For transitions to be effective, they should (1) mention the point just discussed, (2) relate that point to the objective of the talk, and (3) introduce the next point. All three steps are incorporated in the following transition:

> We have discussed the precedents for a mandatory physical fitness program in the military, but these precedents alone will not prove a need for such a program. To more fully understand that need, we must next examine in several practical situations the benefits of mandatory physical fitness.

When planned and used correctly, transitions act as "mini-summaries" and contribute substantially to the continuity of the total talk.

Interim Summaries

Summaries after main points or key ideas are useful tools for maintaining continuity within a talk and for highlighting areas of particular importance. Interim summaries are not always necessary in a talk. In fact, if the point is very clear, a summary may be unnecessarily redundant and boring. You should use them, however, when main points are unusually long or contain complex or unfamiliar information. With interim summaries you repeat information concisely and reinforce audience understanding before new information is presented. Interim summaries should not take the place of transitions; they should provide a means for you to progress logically from one main point, through the transition, and into the next point.

After Preparation, Then What?

The first four chapters of this book have provided suggestions on preparing, organizing, supporting, and finally on beginning and ending the talk. What comes next is the most frightening part for many people—the actual presentation of the talk. The next chapter provides some suggestions for speaking more effectively.

CHAPTER 5

PRESENTING A TALK

Although preparing a talk can be laborious, for many persons the hardest part is the actual presentation of the talk. Questions speakers most often ask are: How many notes should I use? How can I overcome nervousness? What kind of physical behavior is appropriate for me to use when I speak? What if my voice isn't suited to speaking before a group? How can I project sincerity and enthusiasm? Answers to these questions will provide the content for this chapter.

Methods of Presentation

Speakers can use one of four common methods for presentation: (1) speaking from memory, (2) reading from manuscript, (3)

speaking impromptu with no specific preparation, and (4) speaking extemporaneously with, ideally, a great deal of preparation and a limited number of notes. The fourth method usually allows us the most freedom in adjusting to an audience as we speak and is best suited for almost all speaking in the Air Force.

Memorizing

Speaking from memory is the poorest method of delivering talks, and it should be used very sparingly or not at all. While this method may seem to be helpful for persons who cannot think on their feet, the memorized talk is a straitjacket. Such a talk cannot be adapted to the immediate situation or audience reactions. In other words, it does not allow the speaker to adjust to the particular situation. Moreover, the method is almost sure to destroy spontaneity and a sense of communication. The method also requires an inordinate amount of preparation, and the danger of forgetting is ever present.

Manuscript Reading

Reading a talk from a manuscript allows for planning the exact words and phrases to use. But the disadvantages of this method of presentation far outweigh the advantages. Many speakers use the manuscript as a crutch instead of fully thinking through the ideas in the talk. All too often the written talk is regarded simply as an essay to be read aloud. Therefore, the talk is too broad and has language that is too abstract to be understood when presented orally.

If you must read from a manuscript, consider the following suggestions:

Prepare the manuscript.

- Spoken words should be simpler, clearer, and more vivid than writing.

- Sentences should be shorter and ideas less complex than in writing.
- Transitions between thoughts and ideas need to be clear. Provide signposts to keep the audience from getting lost.
- Use repetition to emphasize main ideas and key points.
- Use direct address when speaking about people. Personal pronouns such as *I, we, our, us, you,* are better than *they, people, a person, the reader, the hearer.*
- Use concrete language where possible. Follow abstract or complicated reasoning with specific examples, comparisons, and definitions.

Prepare a reading draft.

- Use as large a type as possible. Special type two or three times larger than ordinary will greatly enhance visibility.
- Double or triple space to make the words stand out more clearly and reduce chance for confusion or misreading of the text.
- Type on only one side of the paper to facilitate handling.
- Mark your manuscript, perhaps using vertical lines between words where you wish to pause. Underscore words you want to emphasize. Some speakers use double and triple vertical lines or underlining for added emphasis.
- Mark places in the manuscript where you plan to use visual aids.
- Use short paragraphs to reduce the chance of losing your place.
- Some speakers vary the length of line according to meaning.

Practice the talk.

- Read the talk aloud to see how it sounds. Recording yourself on a cassette recorder and listening to the playback will help you to discover places where you may not be communicating effectively.
- Read and reread the talk several times, perhaps once a day for several days if you have time.

- Try to make your talk sound like conversation, as if you were thinking the words for the first time as you read them.
- Avoid combinations of words that are difficult to say. Make necessary changes on the manuscript.
- Practice looking at your audience most of the time as the manuscript becomes more familiar to you.
- Provide the punctuation with vocal inflection, variety, and pauses.

Presenting the talk.

Use one of two methods for handling the manuscript. (1) Hold the manuscript in front of you with one hand high enough so that you can see it without bending your head, but not high enough to hide your face. The other hand will be free to turn pages and gesture. (2) Place the manuscript on a speaker's stand or table so that both hands are free to gesture. Make sure, however, that the manuscript is placed high enough to read from without bending over. Sometimes books or other objects may be used to raise the manuscript to the desired height. Whichever method is used, remember to *let the eyes, not the head, drop to the paper.*

- Don't explain why you choose to read the talk. If you have prepared well, you should do a good job and no apologies will be necessary.
- Be willing to change the wording here and there as you go along if it will help you communicate ideas to your hearers. These changes will make delivery more conversational.
- Insert comments of up to a sentence or two in length to add variety, but be careful not to deviate so far from the manuscript that your train of thought is interrupted. You should have carefully thought through and prepared the manuscript. Last minute changes and impromptu asides can be confusing both for you and your hearers.
- Be flexible enough so that you can shorten the talk if necessary.
- Let pauses be dictated by ideas. Pause wherever there would normally be a pause in the same language in informal conversa-

tion. You will need to pause often, even when the written punctuation does not dictate a pause.

● Concentrate on the meaning and ideas rather than on individual words. If you have written your own talk, you are intimate with the ideas and the words you chose to express them. You built the talk, you should understand it. Therefore, the most helpful aid to good delivery is to recreate the feeling that helped you put the words on paper. Speak no passage until its meaning hits your mind.

● Construct the next idea in your mind before uttering it.

● Read with all the sincerity, enthusiasm, directness, and force that is proper to the occasion.

● Use gestures and look directly at the audience when executing them.

A manuscript talk, then, is not, as someone once said, merely "an essay on its hind legs." The manuscript should be written in a conversational tone rather than formal English. It is meant to be heard, not read. If you prepare well, practice diligently, and attend to factors of delivery, you can usually read very acceptably and spontaneously.

Impromptu

Speaking impromptu requires a tremendous amount of skill and knowledge. You may find it necessary at times to talk on the spur of the moment without any preparation. But this method should be used only by experienced speakers who are saturated with their subjects and who have the ability to organize their thoughts for learning as they speak. Even these experienced speakers fall back upon thoughts and phrases they have used before. They have spent years, so to speak, in preparing to give an unprepared talk.

Extemporaneous

The technique effective speakers use most widely, extemporaneous speaking, produces the most fruitful results when it is based upon full preparation and adequate practice. The talk is carefully planned and outlined in detail. The speaker's only guide is usually a well-constructed outline. It is a lesson planned idea by idea rather than word by word.

The advantages of speaking from a well-planned outline are many. The method compels speakers to organize ideas and puts pressure on them to weigh materials in advance. It gives freedom to adapt a talk to the occasion and to adjust to audience reactions. It enables speakers to change what they plan to say right up to the moment of utterance. In short, the extemporaneous method will permit the speaker to adhere to the two vital needs of effective speaking: adequate preparation and a lively sense of communication.

You may want to prepare two versions of the outline. One version will be very complete—almost in manuscript form—so you can return to it several weeks or months later if you are called upon to give a similar talk. Another version will be much briefer—perhaps only one page long, or written on cards so you can use it when you actually give your talk. This brief outline may be thought of as a *keyword* outline with keywords and key phrases to remind you of main points, subpoints, support material you plan to use, questions you might ask, and the things you want to mention in the introduction and conclusion.

Keyword Outline

The keyword outline should be divided into three main parts: introduction, body, and conclusion. As discussed previously, the introduction may have three subparts: attention, motivation, and overview. The body will have the main points of the talk as major subdivisions. The conclusion may have three subdivisions: final summary, remotivation, and closure.

Symbol System. To show the relative importance of lesson materials in the body of the lesson, you might use a number or letter symbol before each entry. Figure 2 gives an example. But some rules of outlining to remember are:

1. Only one symbol should be used per point or idea.
2. Subordinate points should be indented.
3. The principle of subpoints or subordination means that a point follows logically or supports the point above it.

A tentative outline for a talk on nonverbal communication was presented in chapter 2. Consider how that outline might be revised once you have collected all of your material. As you can see from the keyword outline, the speaker plans to seek the audience's attention by using a familiar quotation—"actions speak louder than words"—and then use an example about a "dinner jacket." The speaker plans to provide motivation by giving testimony from an expert concerning the amount of the message that is communicated nonverbally. Then the speaker plans to use a visual aid—an overview chart—that outlines the main points of the talk.

The two main points—know the performance factors of nonverbal communication and know the nonperformance factors of nonverbal communication—are arranged topically. The subpoints under the first main point (upper body, middle body, and lower body) are arranged spatially—from top to bottom. Each of the subsubpoints (head-eyes-facial expression; arms-hands-torso; hips-legs-feet) are also arranged spatially—from top to bottom.

The subpoints under main point 2 (objects, space, and time) are arranged topically. The subsubpoints under objects are arranged according to time, and subsubpoints under space seem to be arranged topically.

Notice also that the speaker has written keywords not only for main points, subpoints, and subsubpoints but also has written enough down to remember the support that will be used. Some speakers also like to write in their suggested transitions. While writing of the transitions may inhibit spontaneity, the practice is often preferable to having weak or no transitions.

Obviously, when preparing your notes for your talk you will want to use what works best for you. This sample outline is only intended as a possible way of preparing your notes.

Sample Keyword Outline

NONVERBAL COMMUNICATION

INTRODUCTION

Attention: "Actions speak louder than words" (dinner jacket example).

Motivation: Dr Ray Birdwhistle (65 percent of message communicated nonverbally). Importance—jobs, family, church, clubs.

Overview: Chart listing main points and first-level subpoints. Define "performance factors" and "nonperformance factors."

BODY

1. Know the performance factors of nonverbal communication.

   a. Upper Body (importance capitalized on by F.D.R.).

      (1) Head.

         (a) Theory of origin of head gesture.
         (b) Cultural differences.

      (2) Eyes (very important).

         (a) Show interest in others (blind student example).
         (b) Nonverbal feedback (cultural differences).
         (c) Increase credibility (describe University of Missouri studies).

      (3) Facial Expression.

         (a) Affect displays (read quote on expression).
         (b) Affect recognition (use everyday examples).

   b. Middle Body.

      (1) Arms (demonstrate how we use them).
      (2) Hands (primary means of gesturing).

         (a) Compare meanings from different cultures (okay and victory signs).
         (b) Demonstrate use of hands.

      (3) Torso (demonstrate shoulder, chest, stomach—belly dancer example).

   c. Lower Body.

      (1) Hips (Elvis example).
      (2) Legs (compare with foundation of building).
      (3) Feet (show different angles).

Figure 2

2. Know the nonperformance factors of nonverbal communication.

  a. Objects.

    (1) Present (clothes, home, office).
    (2) Past (things we have constructed—former home example).

  b. Space.

    (1) Personal.

      (a) Stress cultural differences (contrast US with Korea, Turkey, etc.).
      (b) Space bubble (example of waiting for a bus or in a line).
      (c) Acceptable distance (cite statistics by Hall).

    (2) Constructed (office arrangement, fences, etc.).

  c. Time (humorous definition from *Esquire*, Wetumpka example).

CONCLUSION

Final Summary: Mention main points.

Remotivation: Stress importance of nonverbal to each person.

Closure: Tell humorous story of how deaf man solved problems; challenge listeners to do likewise.

Figure 2 — Continued

Nervousness

If you suffer from stage fright, nervousness, or fear of speaking, your audience may also become uneasy or anxious. Yet some nervousness is both natural and desirable. Even skilled speakers often experience the queasy feeling of "butterflies in the stomach" as they prepare to speak. The secret is to get the butterflies "flying in formation," through practice. Just as a visiting athletic team practices on a field before game time to accustom themselves to differences in terrain and environment, so you may need to dry run or practice your talk several times, preferably in the room where the talk will be given, before actually presenting it. Practice reminds us to look up the pronunciation of a word that is new or check an additional piece of information on an important point.

Suggestions for Nervous Speakers

Consider the following suggestions for coping with nervousness.

1. Enthusiasm is the key when practice is over and you are ready to deliver the talk. At times you may talk on subjects that you find dull, but as you get more involved, the subject becomes more interesting. There is no such thing as a dull subject, only dull speakers. It is important to be enthusiastic about your subject, because enthusiasm can replace fear. And the more enthusiatic you are about the subject, the more involved the audience will be both with you and what you are saying.

2. Hold good thoughts toward your audience. The listeners in the audience are the same ones that you enjoy speaking with in a less structured environment. Most audiences are made up of warm human beings with an interest in what you have to say. They rarely boo or throw vegetables. Most listeners have great empathy for speakers and want them to do a good job.

3. Do not rush as you begin to speak. Many speakers are so anxious to get started that they begin before they are really ready. The little extra time taken to arrange your notes will generally pay big dividends. When you are ready to begin, look at various parts of the audience, take a deep breath, and begin to speak.

Physical Behavior

Communication experts tell us that over half of our meaning may be communicated nonverbally. Although nonverbal meaning is communicated through vocal cues, much meaning is carried by the physical behaviors of eye contact, bodily movement, and gestures. You need to know how these physical behaviors can improve your speaking skill.

Eye Contact

Eye contact is one of the most important factors of nonverbal communication. Nothing will enhance your delivery more than effective eye contact with your audience. Eye contact is important for three reasons. *First*, it lets the listeners know that you are interested in them. Most people like others to look at them when talking. *Second*, effective eye contact allows you to receive non-verbal feedback from your audience. With good eye contact, you can gauge the effect of your remarks. You can determine if you are being understood and which points are making an impact and which are not. You will be able to detect signs of poor understanding and signs that the listeners are losing interest. Then you can adjust your rate of delivery or emphasis. You can rephrase or summarize certain points or add more supporting data. *Third*, effective eye contact enhances your credibility. Speakers with the greatest eye contact are judged by listeners as being more competent.

To achieve genuine eye contact, you must do more than merely look in the direction of your listeners. You must have an earnest desire to communicate with them. The old advice of looking over the tops of your listeners' heads or attempting to look at all parts of the audience systematically simply does not describe effective eye contact. Furthermore, looking at only one part of the audience or directing attention only to those listeners who seem to give you reinforcing feedback may cause you to ignore large parts of the audience. Make it evident to each person in a small group and each part of the audience in larger auditoriums that you are interested in them as individuals and eager to have them understand the ideas you are presenting. In this way you will establish mental as well as sensory contact with your listeners.

Effective eye contact can be described as *direct* and *impartial*. You look directly into the eyes of your listeners, and you look impartially at all parts of the audience, not just at a chosen few.

Body Movement

Body movement is one of the important factors of dynamic and meaningful physical behavior. Good body movement is important because it catches the eye of the listener. It helps to hold the attention needed for good communication. But movement can also represent a marked departure or change in your delivery pattern—a convenient way of punctuating and paragraphing your message. Listeners will know that you are finished with one idea or line of thought and ready to transition to the next. Finally, aside from its effects on the listeners, movement helps you as a lecturer. It helps you work off excess energy that can promote nervousness. Movement puts you at ease.

How much movement is desirable? Some speakers never move yet are quite effective. However unless the formality of the situation or the need to use a fixed microphone keeps you in one position, then you probably should move frequently. Movement from behind the lectern can reduce the psychological distance between you and your listeners and place them more at ease. Some speakers feel that they need the lectern to hold their notes. But in most cases it is actually more effective if you carry your notes with you rather than looking down at the lectern to see them. But whenever you look at your notes, remember to *drop your eyes not your head*. In other words, have your notes high enough that you can see them.

Of course, some speakers move too much. Perhaps out of nervousness they pace back and forth in front of the audience. Still others have awkward movement that does not aid communication. Some leave their notes on the lectern then move in and out from behind it like a hula dancer. Others plant their feet firmly in one place then rock from one side to the other in regular cadence.

Effective body movement can be described as *free* and *purposeful*. You should be free to move around in front of the listeners. You should not feel restrained to stay behind the lectern but should move with reason and purpose. Use your movement to punctuate, direct attention, and otherwise aid communication.

Gestures

Gestures may be used to clarify or emphasize ideas. By gestures we mean the purposeful use of the hands, arms, shoulders, and head to reinforce what is being said. Fidgeting with a paper clip, rearranging and shuffling papers, and scratching your ear are not gestures. They are not purposeful and they distract from the verbal message. Placing both hands in your pockets, or behind your back, or in front of you in a fig leaf position severely limits their use for gesturing. Holding your shoulders and head in one position during the talk will also rob you of an effective means of strengthening your communication.

Although gestures can be perfected through practice, they will be most effective if you make a conscious effort to relax your muscles before you speak, perhaps by taking a few short steps or unobtrusively arranging your notes. Effective gestures are complete and vigorous. Many speakers begin to gesture, but perhaps out of fear, they do not carry through and their gestures abort. Comedians get laughs from the audience by timing gestures improperly. A gesture that comes after the word or phrase is spoken appears ludicrous. Good gestures should come exactly at the time or slightly before the point is made verbally. Poor timing results from attempting to ''can'' or preplan gestures. Finally, good gestures are versatile. A stereotyped gesture will not fit all subjects and situations. Furthermore, the larger the audience, the more pronounced the gestures will need to be. As with all aspects of communication, gestures must fit the situation.

You should not adopt a dynamic, forceful mode of delivery if by nature you are quiet and reserved. As with movement, gestures should spring from within. Effective gestures are both *natural* and *spontaneous*. Observe persons talking with each other in a small group. You should try to approximate the same naturalness and spontaneity of gestures when you are speaking.

Use of Voice

A good voice has three important characteristics. It is reasonably pleasant, it is easily understood, and it expresses differences in meaning. Technically we might label these three properties as quality, intelligibility, and variety.

Quality

Quality refers to the overall impression a voice makes on others. Certainly a pleasing quality or tone is a basic component of a good speaking voice. Some persons have a full rich quality, others one that is shrill and nasal, and still others may have a breathy and muffled tone or quality. Although basic aspects of quality may be difficult to change, your voice may become more breathy when you are excited, tense when suspense is involved, and resonant when reading solemn language. Listeners can often tell from the voice if the speaker is happy, angry, sad, fearful, or confident. Similarly vocal quality can convey sincerity and enthusiasm. Some speakers are overly concerned about the basic quality of their voices, but at the same time they pay too little attention to the effect of attitude and emotion on the voice. Most people have reasonably pleasant voices that are suitable for speaking.

Intelligibility

Intelligibility or understandability of your speech depends on several factors.

1. Articulation refers to the precision and clarity with which sounds of speech are uttered. A synonym of articulation is enunciation. Good articulation is chiefly the job of the jaw, tongue, and lips. Most articulation problems result from laziness of the tongue and lips or failure to open the mouth wide enough. You should overarticulate rather than underarticulate your speech sounds. What sounds like overarticulation to you will come out as crisp, understandable words and phrases to your listeners.

2. Pronunciation refers to the traditional or customary utterance of words. Standards of pronunciation differ, making it difficult at times to know what is acceptable. Dictionaries are useful, but as they become outdated, they should not be adhered to excessively. Generally, educated people in your community as well as national radio and television announcers provide a good standard for pronunciation. Common faults of pronunciation are to misplace the accent (saying *de*-vice instead of de-*vice*), to omit

sounds (guh/mnt for government), to add sounds (ath*a*lete for athlete), and to sound silent letters (mor*t*gage or of*t*en). Do not overcompensate to the point that you call attention to your speech, but remember that pronunciation acceptable in informal conversation may be substandard when speaking in front of a group.

3. Vocalized pause is the name we give to syllables "a," "uh," "um," and "ah" often at the beginning of a sentence. While a few vocalized pauses are natural and do not distract, too many impede the communication process.

4. Overuse of stock expressions such as "OK," "like," and "you know" should be avoided. These expressions serve no positive communicative function and only convey a lack of originality by the speaker.

5. Substandard grammar has no place in speaking. It will only serve to reduce your credibility with some listeners. Research shows that even persons who have been using substandard grammar all of their lives can, with diligent practice, make significant gains in this area in a relatively short time.

Variety

Variety is the spice of speaking. Listeners tire rapidly when listening to a speaker who doesn't vary delivery style or a speaker who has a monotonous voice. A speaker's voice that is intelligible and of good quality may still not appeal to listeners. You may vary your voice and at the same time improve the communication by considering the vocal fundamentals of rate, volume, force, pitch, and emphasis.

1. Most people speak at a rate of from 100 to 180 words a minute when presenting a talk. In normal speech, however, we vary the rate often so that even within the 100- to 180-word constraints there is much change. The temperamentally excitable person may speak at a rapid rate all the time, and the stolid person generally talks in a slow drawl. The enthusiastic but confident individual, however, will vary the rate of delivery to emphasize ideas and feelings. A slower rate may be appropriate

for presenting main points, while a more rapid rate may lend itself to support material. The experienced speaker also knows that an occasional pause punctuates thought and emphasizes ideas. A dramatic pause at the proper time may express feelings and ideas even more effectively than words.

2. Volume is important to the speaker. Always be certain that all the audience can hear you. Nothing hinders the effect of a talk more than to have some listeners unable to hear. On the other hand, the talk should not be too loud for a small room. A bombastic or overly loud speaker tires listeners out very quickly.

3. Force is needed at times to emphasize and dramatize ideas. A drowsy audience will come to attention quickly if the speaker uses force effectively. At times a sudden reduction in force may be as effective as a rapid increase. By learning to control the force of your voice, you can help to add emphasis and improve communication.

4. Pitch is the highness or lowness of the voice. All things being equal, a higher pitched voice carries better than a low pitched one. On the other hand, listeners will tend to tire faster when listening to the higher pitched voice. If your voice is within normal limits—neither too high nor too low—work for variety as you speak.

5. Emphasis obviously stems from all forms of vocal variety, and any change in rate, force, or pitch will influence the emphasis. The greater or more sudden the change, the greater the emphasis will be. As a speaker you will want to use emphasis wisely. Two things should be avoided: *over*emphasis and *continual* emphasis. Be judicious. Emphasizing a point beyond its real value may cause you to lose credibility with your listeners.

Sincerity

Ironically, one of the most important points to be discussed in this chapter can be covered with just a few words. A speaker certainly needs to prepare well and possess strong delivery skills to do an effective job in front of a group. But something more is

71

needed. To be really effective, a speaker must be sincere. So long as you obviously try to generate light and not merely heat, listeners will be amazingly tolerant of weaknesses in both preparation and delivery. But give them a chance to suspect your sincerity, and you lose effectiveness. And once lost, effectiveness is nearly impossible to regain. What is sincerity? Sincerity may be defined as a state of appearing to be without deceit, pretense, or hypocrisy—a state of honesty, truthfulness, and faithfulness.

Sincerity toward your listeners is reflected in your eye contact, enthusiasm, and concern about audience members as individuals. Sincerity toward the subject is judged by whether or not you seem involved and interested in the subject or topic of the talk. Sincerity toward self is displayed in the confidence and concern you have that you are doing the best job possible. Lack of sincerity in any of these areas will, almost certainly, directly hinder communication.